Rookie
Read-About
H

Martin Luther King Jr. Day

by Lisa M. Herrington

Content Consultants

Nanci R. Vargus, Ed.D.
Professor Emeritus, University of Indianapolis

Carrie A. Bell, MST Visual Arts – All Grades
Julia A. Stark Elementary School, Stamford, Connecticut

Reading Consultant

Jeanne M. Clidas, Ph.D.
Reading Specialist

Children's Press®
An Imprint of Scholastic Inc.
New York Toronto London Auckland Sydney
Mexico City New Delhi Hong Kong
Danbury, Connecticut

Library of Congress Cataloging-in-Publication Data
Herrington, Lisa M.
  Martin Luther King Jr. day / by Lisa M. Herrington.
     pages cm. — (Rookie read-about holidays)
  Includes index.
  ISBN 978-0-531-27205-3 (library binding) — ISBN 978-0-531-27355-5 (pbk.)
  1. Martin Luther King, Jr., Day—Juvenile literature. I. Title.

E185.97.K5H47 2013

 394.261—dc23   2013014852

Produced by Spooky Cheetah Press

Printed in China 62

SCHOLASTIC, CHILDREN'S PRESS, ROOKIE READ-ABOUT®, and associated logos
are trademarks and/or registered trademarks of Scholastic Inc.

1 2 3 4 5 6 7 8 9 10 R 23 22 21 20 19 18 17 16 15 14

Photographs © 2014: Adam Chinitz: 28; AP Images: 12 (Atlanta Journal-
Constitution), cover, 19, 30 bottom, 31 center top; Corbis Images: 15, 30 top, 31
center bottom (Bettmann), 31 bottom (Flip Schulke); Everett Collection: 8, 11, 16;
Louise Gardner: 7; Media Bakery/Ariel Skelley: 23; Polaris Images/Molly Riley:
27; Shutterstock, Inc.: 3 top (Neftali), 3 bottom (Rudy Balasko); Superstock, Inc./
Frances M. Roberts/Ambient Images Inc.: 4; The Image Works/Jeff Greenberg: 24;
Thinkstock/Creatas: 20, 31 top.

Table of Contents

LOS ANGELES · MEMPHIS · MONTGOMERY · MIAM

ATLANTA · BIRMINGHAM · DALLAS · DETROIT · JACKSON · LITTLE ROCK

Dr. Martin Luther King, Jr. 1929–1968 · In Memoriam

DR. MARTIN LUTHER KING JR.

MLK
COMMEMORATIV
WALK

4

A Great Leader

Martin Luther King Jr. was an important **leader**. He wanted all people to be treated fairly. He worked to improve the lives of African Americans.

These students are marching in a parade to honor Martin Luther King Jr.

On the third Monday in January, we celebrate Martin Luther King Jr. Day. It is a day to remember how Dr. King worked to make the world a better place.

The date of Martin Luther King Jr. Day changes every year. But it is always celebrated around King's birthday—January 15.

JANUARY

SUNDAY	MONDAY	TUESDAY	WEDNESDAY	THURSDAY	FRIDAY	SATURDAY
			1	2	3	4
5	6	7	8	9	10	11
12	13	14	15	16	17	18
19	20	21	22	23	24	25
26	27	28	29	30	31	

How It Began

Many Americans saw Dr. King as a hero. They wanted to honor him. In 1983, Martin Luther King Jr. Day was made a holiday. It first took place in 1986.

President Ronald Reagan made Martin Luther King Jr. Day an official holiday.

9

Dr. King was born in Georgia in 1929. When he was growing up, black people in the South did not have the same rights as white people. They could not go to the same schools. They had to use different restrooms and water fountains.

FAST FACT!

Dr. King never forgot what his mother told him when he was a boy: "You are as good as anyone."

COLORED

11

Dr. King spent his life helping others. Like his father and grandfather, he became a **minister**. Dr. King and his wife, Coretta Scott, had four children. Dr. King wanted a better life for his kids.

FAST FACT!

Dr. King was very smart. He skipped two grades in high school and started college when he was just fifteen.

Dr. King believed all people should have the same freedoms. In the 1950s and 1960s, he worked hard to change unfair laws. He used peaceful ways. Dr. King led **marches**. He also gave powerful speeches.

Dr. King led many marches to try to change unfair laws.

In Montgomery, Alabama, African Americans had to sit in the back of the bus. In 1955, Dr. King helped put together a plan. African Americans would stop riding buses. The bus companies lost a lot of money. About one year later, the law was changed.

Dr. King rode a Montgomery bus soon after the law was changed.

In 1963, Dr. King led a big march in Washington, D.C. There, he gave his famous "I Have a Dream" speech. In the speech, he said:

"I have a dream that my four little children will one day live in a nation where they will not be judged by the color of their skin but by the content of their character."

Dr. King gave his speech at the foot of the Lincoln Memorial. Abraham Lincoln was the president who put an end to slavery in the United States.

Children of all races can now attend the same schools.

Dr. King's hard work made a difference. New laws that protected **civil rights** were passed. Those laws made sure that all Americans are treated equally.

The Nobel Peace Prize is an important award. Each year, it is given to someone who works for peace. In 1964, Dr. King received the award for his civil rights work.

Honoring Dr. King's Dream

Today we honor Dr. King in many ways. Children learn about the civil rights leader in school. They do projects that celebrate his life and work.

These students are giving a report on Martin Luther King Jr.

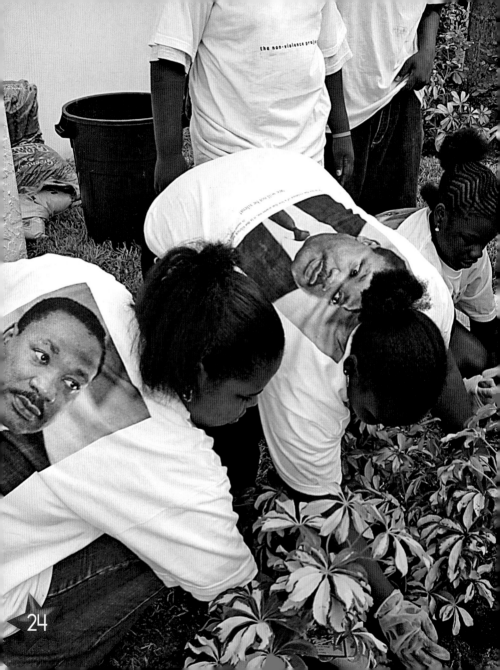

Many people consider Martin Luther King Jr. Day a day "on" instead of a day off. Some kids do volunteer work. Some clean up parks. Others help the homeless. Like Dr. King, they want to make the world a better place.

These students are creating a community garden to improve their neighborhood.

In 2011, the Martin Luther King Jr. Memorial opened in Washington, D.C. Many people visit it on this special holiday to celebrate the life of this great leader.

The King memorial is located near where he gave his "I Have a Dream" speech.

I WAS A

Make a Dream Display

What You'll Need

- White paper plate
- Glue stick
- Glitter
- Crayons or markers
- Hole punch
- Yarn

Directions

1. With an adult's help, use the glue stick to make a peace sign in the center of the paper plate. Cover with glitter and shake off excess over a trash can.

2. Ask an adult to help you write your dream for a better world around the outer rim of the paper plate.

3. Add other decorations until your project is complete.

4. Punch a hole in the top of the plate. String the yarn through to make a loop and tie a knot on top.

5. Hang your dream display where you can always see it.

Show What You Know!

- How does the photo below show how Martin Luther King Jr. worked for equal rights for all people?
- Write a sentence to describe what is happening in the picture.
- What makes someone a good leader?
- How was Martin Luther King Jr. a good leader?

I Have a Dream

- Reread the text from Martin Luther King Jr.'s "I Have a Dream" speech on page 18.
- In your own words, describe his dream.

30

Glossary

civil rights (SI-vuhl rites): equal treatment for all Americans under the law

leader (LEE-duhr): a person who is in charge

marches (MARCH-es): large groups of people walking together to express a strong opinion about something

minister (MIN-uh-stur): someone who leads a church

Index

Facts for Now

Visit this Scholastic Web site for more information on
Martin Luther King Jr. Day:
www.factsfornow.scholastic.com
Enter the keywords **Martin Luther King Jr.**

About the Author

Lisa M. Herrington is a freelance writer and editor. She especially loves writing for children. Lisa lives in Trumbull, Connecticut, with her husband, Ryan, and her daughter, Caroline.